GERALDINE RYAN-LUSH

MRS. CLOHIGGLEDY'S CLUTTER

THE STORY OF A HOARDER

by Geraldine Ryan-Lush

Mulberry Books 2016

ISBN 978-0-9947339-1-7

For Lyla Jean

Mrs. Clohiggledy loved her clutter. She had clutter coming from her walls and ceilings. She had clutter dangling from tops of cupboards. She had clutter curling out of open bureau drawers.

She had clutter clattering in her sinks. She had clutter covering all her lampshades and flower pots and curtain rods and picture frames. Sometimes she painted pictures of her clutter, and gave them away:

Everyone wanted a still life!

And a memory of a trip to Vegas.

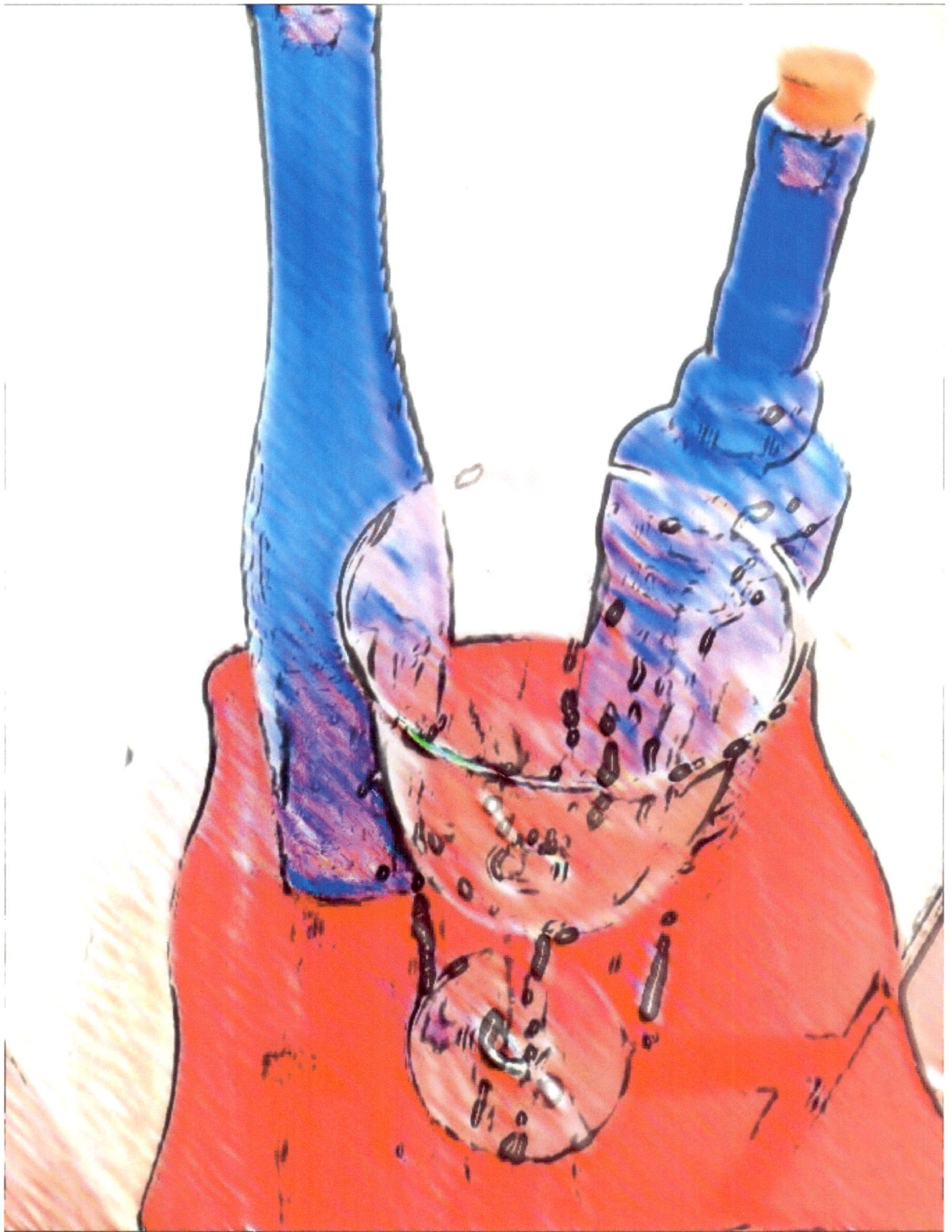

And they loved her Diamond Point Indiana Flash!

Mrs. C couldn't get enough books!

And she loved sketching little tables for her friends!

Her Southern Belles struck a striking pose!

And when she couldn't find enough room for her jewellery and baubles, she draped them on the walls of her bedroom:

"All the better to see them with." She smiled, as she hung each one over a pushpin and went to look for STILL more clutter!   Mrs. Clohoggledy had clutter coming out of everything except her ears, and if she had the room, she would have clutter coming out of her ears, too!

And as you can see, Mrs. Clohiggledy LOVED HATS!

It didn't start out that way. Mrs. Clohiggledy didn't always have clutter. She loved her nice, spacious, minimalist apartment when she moved in. But one day the Superintendent knocked on her door.

"I'm sorry, Mrs. Clohiggledy." He said. "But there are new rules: NO PETS ALLOWED.

So Mrs. Clohiggledy had to give away her Pandora Poodles she had for ten years.

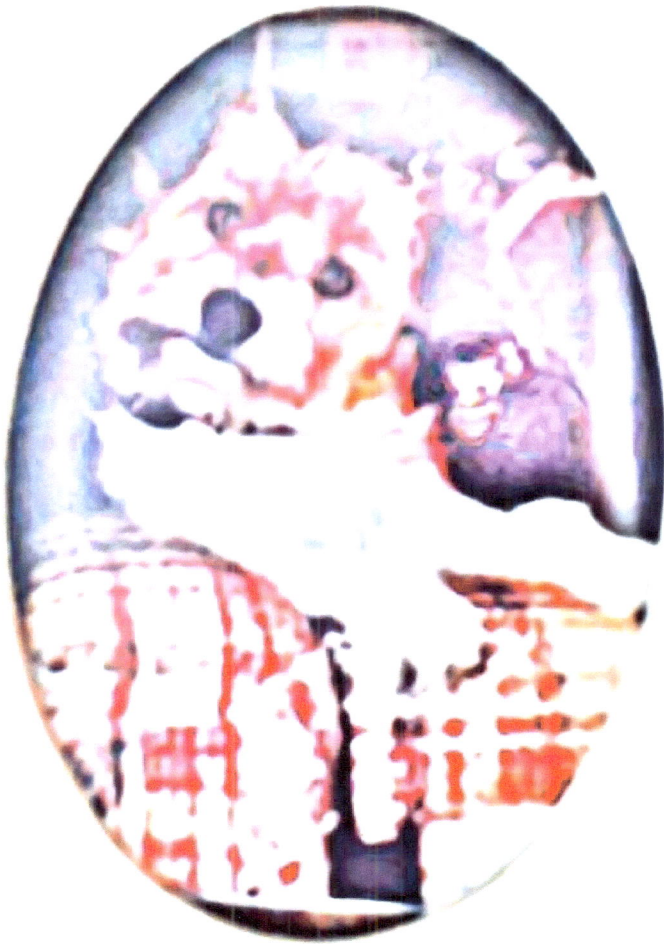

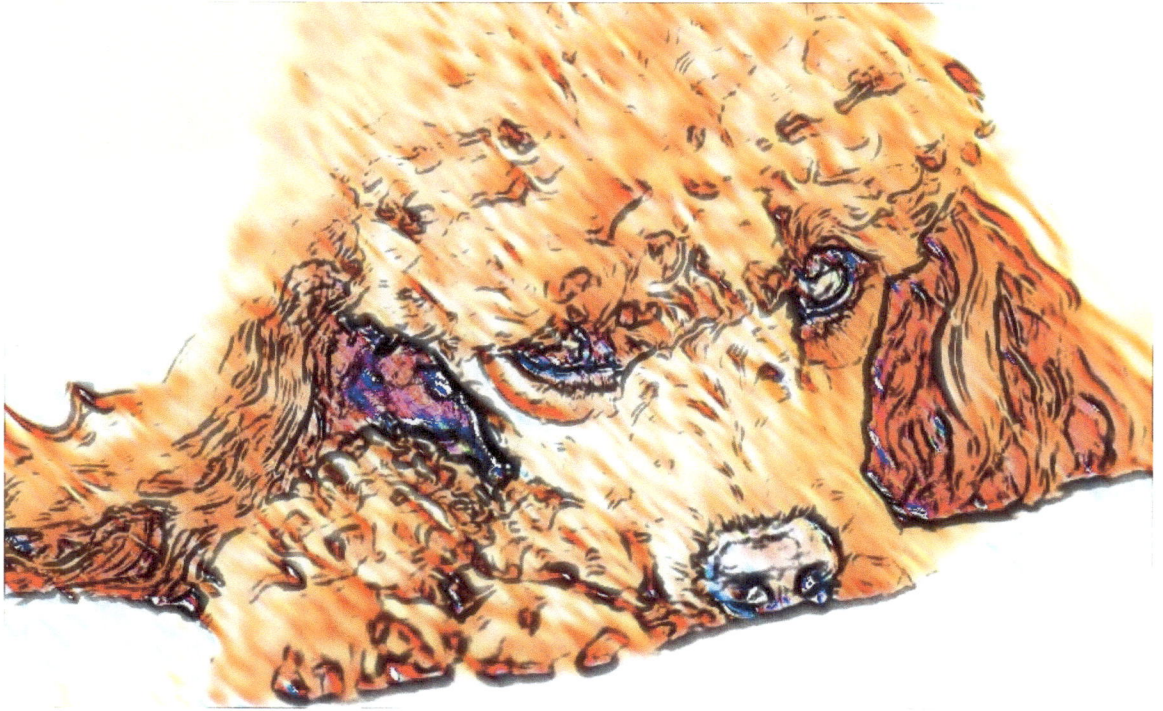

She had to give away her Bad Budgies too because they chattered and sang so loudly to each other, the neighbour who worked night shift downstairs complained.

This made her so sad that she went out and bought a brand new recliner that she could sit in and listen to calming music, while she looked at pictures of her Pandora Poodles and Bad Budgies that she had for ten years.

Things couldn't get any worse for Mrs. Clohiggledy. But they did.

Imelda her daughter got fed up teaching in the city, and moved to New Zealand for excitement. Mrs. Clohiggledy missed HER so much she went out and bought a brand new sofa set on which she could stretch her legs while she had her tea, and chatted to Imelda from New Zealand on Skype.

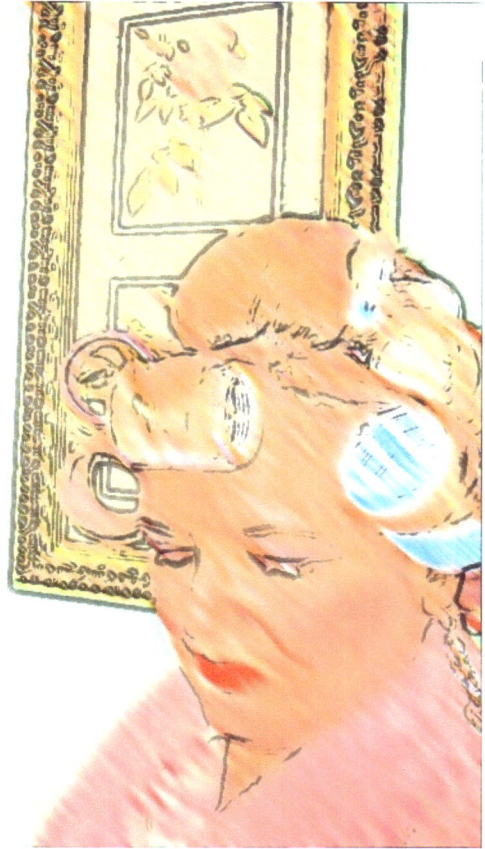

 But not for long. Imelda soon met a friendly and strapping sheep farmer, with an accent to die for, and lo and behold, she got married in the Land Down Under, and Mrs. Clohiggledy sure wasn't going to fly two days underneath the world to see her for a cup of tea and a chat. Not on your life!

So Mrs. Clohiggledy looked around her not-so-spacious, not-so-minimalist apartment anymore. She had enough chairs. She had enough sofas. She had enough tables and cabinets and bookcases and whatnots.

What Mrs. Clohiggledy needed now were enough THINGS to put in those tables and cabinets and bookcases and whatnots; and have lots of STIMULATION so she wouldn't be lonely without Imelda who married the Man From Down Under, and Pandora Poodles and Bad Budgies she had to give away.

But Mrs. Clohiggledy wasn't getting any younger, and she needed to look after her money. Then, one day a bright new message flashed on her computer screen: Fifty Per Cent Off At Magic Village today!" The message flashed in bouncy colored balls and twinkling stars. "It's your special day!"

Look What's Happening!

"Oh my!" said Mrs. Clohiggledy, who couldn't believe her eyes. "I haven't seen this store before. And Fifty Percent Off! Too cool!" Mrs. Clohiggledy hadn't known that everything there was gently used; and a fraction of store prices anyway; and with *Fifty Percent Off along with that?!!* Oh My!!

So Mrs. Clohiggledy got dressed in a nice, vibrant outfit with earrings to match. She took a selfie.

Or two.

Or three.

    Then she got into her Economic-On-Gas Kia and drove to the store with the Fifty Percent Off sign. She stayed for three hours, with a half hour break at the lovely coffee shop across the street. She was in browsing heaven!

The next day, she took off again. MORE stores! MORE sales! MORE treasures!

She bought *Chubby Cherub* vases. She bought *Fenton Glass Figurines.*
She bought *Imperial Glass Candlewick.* She bought *Jeannette Glass
Carnival* and *Diamond Point Indiana,* with castors to match! She bought
Wedgewood and *Currier & Ives* and *Waterford Crystal.*   And all for five
dollars and less! Mrs. Clohiggledy filled her cart. She chatted happily
with the other customers, but kept a sharp eye out for people she *knew,*
because she was a very proud lady, and didn't want people to know she
shopped in those.....you know....*places.*

Mrs. Clohiggledy drove happily home in her Gas-Economic Kia, and laid down her packages. While she brewed and drank her favourite tea, she lovingly fingered each treasure she had bought so modestly.

To Mother
With Love

"My! My!" She exclaimed. "These are collectors' items! And for five or ten dollars! Who would have thought! What a place to shop!"

 Then Mrs. Clohiggledy arranged her treasures in all her cabinets with the glass doors, and lights which shone on them and made them sparkle, and she smiled.

"How beautiful!" She told her jewellery-bedecked walls.   "How simply beautiful!"

That was it for Mrs. Clohiggledy. She was hooked. She began searching out every Garage Sale and Flea Market and Auction and Boot Sale there ever was.

She put a lot of gas in her Gas-Economic-Kia.

She wore a lot of vibrant outfits with earrings to match.

She was running out of space , but that didn't stop her. The neighbours were whispering behind her back. She was a little odd, they said.   They wouldn't help her with her packages anymore. The Superintendent would leave notes under her door. He wouldn't come in, he said. He was afraid he'd break a leg tripping in her clutter.

And the neighbours kept tittering and gossiping.

One day, when Mrs. Clohiggledy had nowhere to put her clutter except in her fridge, she went to an Auction. An enchanting set of *Princess Cordelia* Cottage Ware caught her eye. She had to have them! She waved her poster madly and started bidding. A loud man from the back was bidding higher. And higher. And higher. Mrs. Clohiggledy was getting irritated.

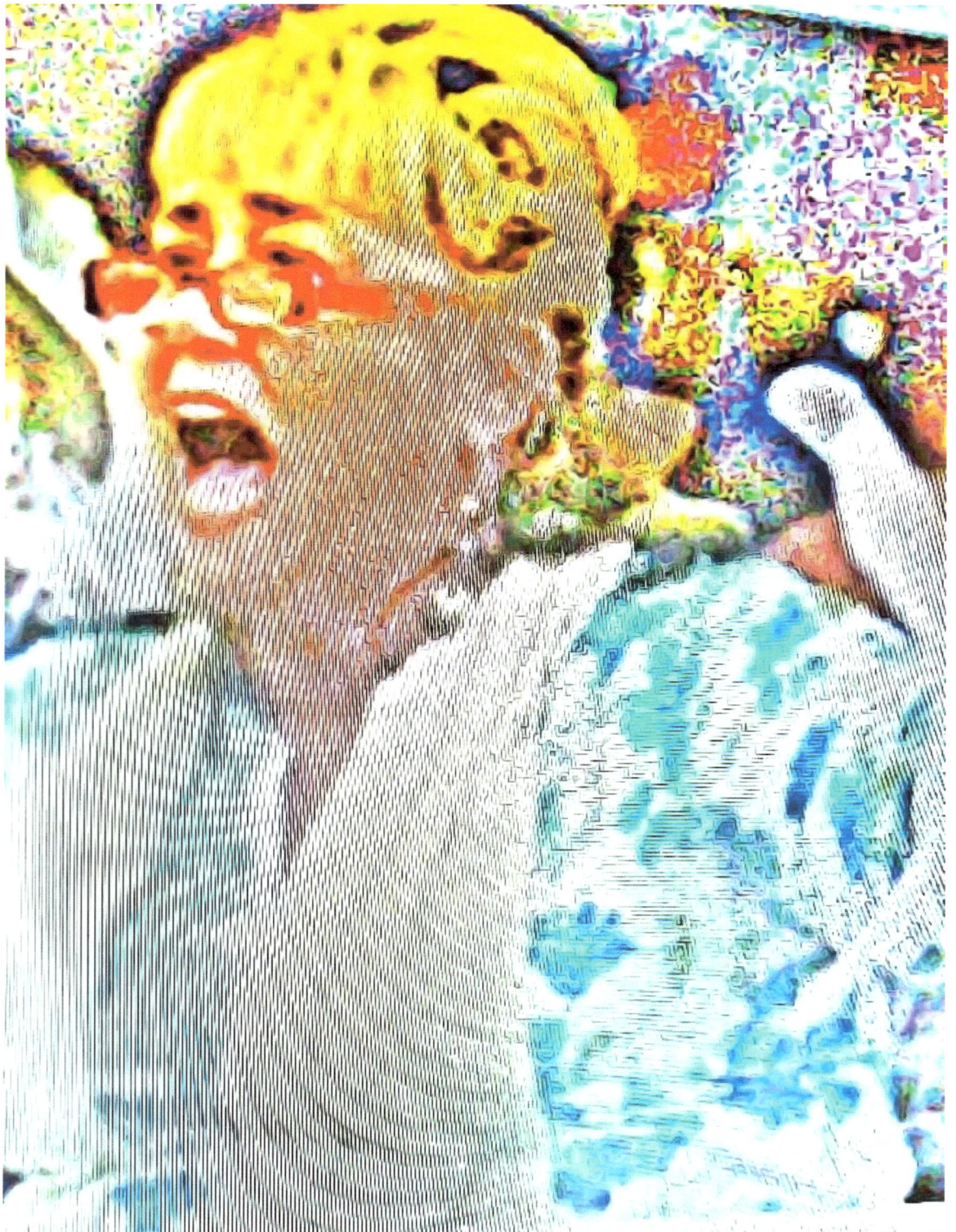

"Five hundred dollars!" She screamed, glaring at the man with an evil eye. Now she would have to sell her Gas-Economic Kia.

"Five hundred and twenty-five dollars!" Yelled the big man back. He had grey hair and intelligent spectacles.

"Six hundred dollars!" Mrs. Clohiggledy screeched. She was very peeved. No one was going to outfox *her*. Especially someone with a loud, strange-sounding voice. How dare this....this....*upstart* think he knew more than she did about Princess Cordelia Cottage Ware. The nerve!

The auctioneer's hammer banged. "Sold! To the lady in the green outfit and matching earrings." Mrs. Clohiggledy started to preen triumphantly. Then she heard THE VOICE again.

"Congratulations." The man said. "You have a good eye." Mrs. Clohiggledy tilted her head. She listened again. An accent to die for. Why, he's from New Zealand!" She said to herself. Mrs. Clohiggledy stopped preening triumphantly and walked over to the big man who also had been a sheep farmer but now went to Auctions. They talked and talked. They talked about Imelda and the Land Down Under. They talked about *Chubby Cherub* and *Imperial Glass Candlewick,* and *Diamond Point Indiana.* With castors to match. They talked about *Wedgewood* and *Currier & Ives,* and *Waterford Crystal.* They even talked about *Princess Cordelia Cottage Ware*, and she didn't give him the evil eye.

They went to more Auctions. They went to Art Galleries and Dinner and the Theatre and Dancing. He shoveled her Gas-Economic-Kia. Then they went on trips to the Land Down Under. They went on many trips.

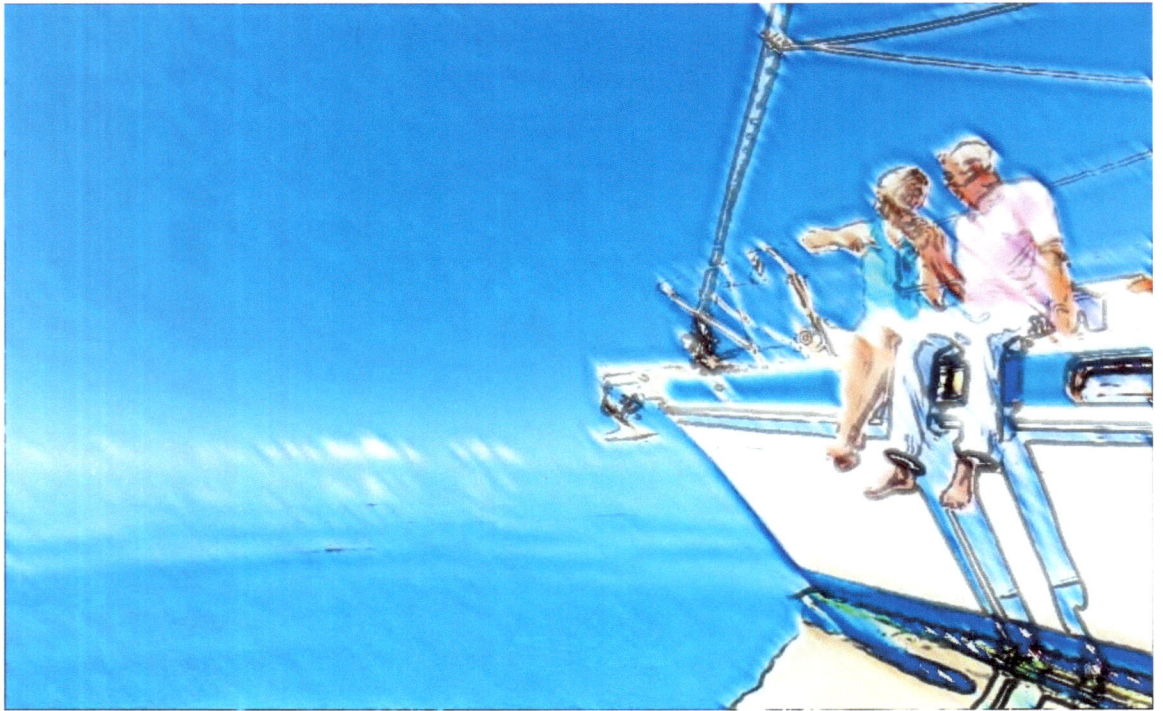

One day Mrs. Clohiggledy got the shock of her life. A watercolour she had painted of some of her clutter sold at auction for fifty thousand dollars!

Sold: Fifty Thousand dollars!

Mrs. Clohiggledy bought a new Gas-Economic-Kia. And she held on to her clutter everyone told her to give away. She gives half of her art money to worthy causes. Now she has a strapping, grey-haired antique dealer with an accent to die for, her clutter to paint pictures of, and a little Grandchild bouncing around, with the same friendly eyes and an accent to die for. Mrs. Clohiggledy is one happy lady.

But Mrs. Clohiggledy still wears a lot of vibrant outfits with earrings to match.   Because you can't keep a stylin' lady down!

No, you can't keep a stylin' lady down!

The End.

Books by Geraldine Ryan-Lush:

-Jeremy Jeckles Hates Freckles (Age 5-10)

-Hairs On Bears   (Age 3-8)

-Poils Poils Et Repoils   (Age 3-8)

-Malcolm The Klutz   (MG Novel)

-Malcolm and The Hamster Lady (MG Novel)

-No Go Potty (MG Novel)

-Hannigan's Hand (Paranormal/Ghost Novel (YA-Adult)

-Hannigan's Hand: The Ghost Woman Talks (Paranormal/Ghost Novel (YA-Adult)

-Once When I Wasn't Looking (Poetry Collection. YA-Adult)

Plus, many other published stories soon to come in book form!

ABOUT THE AUTHOR

Geraldine Ryan-Lush, B.A. Ed., grew up in St. Joseph's, St. Mary's Bay, NL, Canada. She was a classroom teacher and print columnist before becoming a full-time writer. Her books have been on the American Bookseller's Pick Of The Lists, reviewed in School Library Journal, New York, and received the Merit Magazine Studio Award, and Alcuin Society Design Award, among others. They have been reviewed by prestigious sources in the children's literature field, and are in numerous schools and public libraries worldwide, as well as the trades market. She has also been awarded major writing Grants from the Canada Council For The Arts, and the Newfoundland/Labrador Arts Council to further her work. She makes her home in St. John's, NL, Canada.

Contact:

www.mulberrybooks.com   facebook.com/AuthorGeraldineRyanLush

Twitter: @GRyanLush   E-mail: geraldine1942@live.com

Tel: 709.368.5156

www.ingramcontent.com/pod-product-compliance
Lightning Source LLC
Chambersburg PA
CBHW041425090426

42741CB00002B/40